First Questions and Answers about Neighborhoods

Who Named My Street Magnolia?

TIME LIFE for Children ®

ALEXANDRIA, VIRGINIA

Contents

What does a neighborhood look like?

That depends on where it is. A neighborhood is a place where people live close together. In big cities, neighborhoods have tall buildings and busy streets. Outside of cities, neighborhoods have houses and smaller buildings.

5

Who needs neighbors?

We all do. Neighbors are the people you see almost every day. Some neighbors are the children who like to play with you. Others are grownups who are there to lend you and your family a helping hand.

Try it!
How many of your neighbors do you know? Have someone help you make a list of their names.

Why do we separate our garbage?

In some neighborhoods, people separate the trash that can be recycled, or used over again. Newspapers can be made into more paper. Cans and bottles can be used over or made into other useful things. People take paper, cans, and bottles to recycling centers, or leave them out for trucks to pick up.

Did you know?
Paper is made from trees. When you recycle newspapers, you save trees from being cut down.

9

Who takes the garbage away?

Some trash cannot be recycled. That is why garbage trucks drive through the neighborhood once or twice a week. The workers collect bags filled with trash and toss them into their truck. A large blade in the truck crushes the garbage so it all fits inside.

11

Who else works around here?

There are lots of jobs to be done in a neighborhood.

Gardeners trim trees and care for grass.

Newspaper carriers deliver papers.

Bus drivers take people from one place to another.

Truckdrivers deliver everything from fuel for heat to diapers for babies.

Ice cream vendors sell treats to children.

Chimney sweeps clean chimneys.

13

How does the mail carrier know where I live?

Every letter you receive has your address on it. Your name, the name of your street, the number of your house or apartment, and the town where you live all make up your address.

423 Candlewood Ln.
Leawood, Ks. 66206

Jacob Price
2315 Magnolia St.
Shelby, N.C. 28150

Try it!

You can start a collection with the different stamps that come in the mail. Have a parent help you paste them in a notebook. Add to your collection every day.

The mail carrier goes from one address to the next. At each stop she drops off the letters and packages for the people who live there.

Who named my street Magnolia?

The people who planned your neighborhood selected its street names. Often they choose tree and flower names, like Walnut Lane or Magnolia Street. Columbus Road and Washington Avenue are named for famous people. First Avenue and Third Street have numbers for names.

Some street names tell you about a place. River Road may run along a river. Main Street is often the busiest one in town.

16

WALNUT LANE

MAGNOLIA STREET

Try it!
Do you know your whole address? Practice telling it to a parent.

17

What are the other signs in my neighborhood for?

The streets near your home are busy places. Signs help make sure things go smoothly for everyone.

These are some signs you will find around the neighborhood. How many of each one can you find here?

STOP
Cars stop here and wait until it is safe to go.

BIKE ROUTE
Bikers can ride safely along streets marked with this sign.

NO PARKING
Cars are not allowed to park here.

ONE WAY
Cars can go only the way the arrow is pointing.

CROSSWALK
Children can cross the street safely near this sign.

19

Where can I go to play?

Neighborhoods with lots of children usually have playgrounds with swings, slides, and climbing equipment. Here are some safety rules to follow at the playground: Always go with friends or family; be sure to hold on tight when climbing; and never walk in front of a swing.

20

What happens in a post office?

Letters and packages are sent all over the world. At the counter, a clerk weighs each package and stamps it. In the back room, workers sort letters and packages. The mail is sent to other post offices by truck, plane or train. When it arrives, a mail carrier delivers it.

Try it!

Do you know someone who lives far away? Draw a picture and ask a parent to mail it to that person. How long do you think it will take to get there?

4.2 lbs. $3.98

23

Why do libraries have so many books?

Because people want to know about so many different things. A library lets everyone share books. People take turns using thousands of books–many more than one family could own. Libraries also have newspapers, magazines, videos, and tapes.

EXTRA! EXTRA!
READ ALL ABOUT IT!

Ask the librarian how you can get your own library card today.

STRETCH YOUR

IMAGINATION—READ

25

Is school fun?

School can be lots of fun. It is a great place to make friends with children from all over the neighborhood. School is also a place to learn about things like letters, words, and numbers. Sometimes classes go on special trips to visit places like farms, museums, and zoos.

Why is that man wearing a bright vest?

He's a crossing guard. His vest makes it easy for drivers to see him when he stops cars in the street.

Crossing guards stand at busy crosswalks before and after school. While children wait on the sidewalk, the guard steps into the road. He blows a whistle, uses hand signals, or holds up a sign to stop traffic. Then the children can cross the street safely.

28

What are those wires for?

They bring power into people's homes. Some wires make telephones work. Others carry electricity for things like light bulbs, fans, and radios. In some neighborhoods, cable wires carry signals to your television.

31

What happens at a gas station?

Giant tanks filled with gasoline are underneath the station. The gasoline travels through pipes from the underground tanks to the gas pump. Then it squirts into your car's gas tank.

Workers called mechanics fix cars at service stations. When a car breaks down, a tow truck brings it in for repairs.

Why do some streets have parking meters?

In city neighborhoods, drivers often must pay to leave their cars along the street. When a coin drops into a parking meter, an arrow shows how long the car can be parked–usually an hour or two. If a red flag pops up in the meter's window, the car has been there too long. The driver may get a parking ticket.

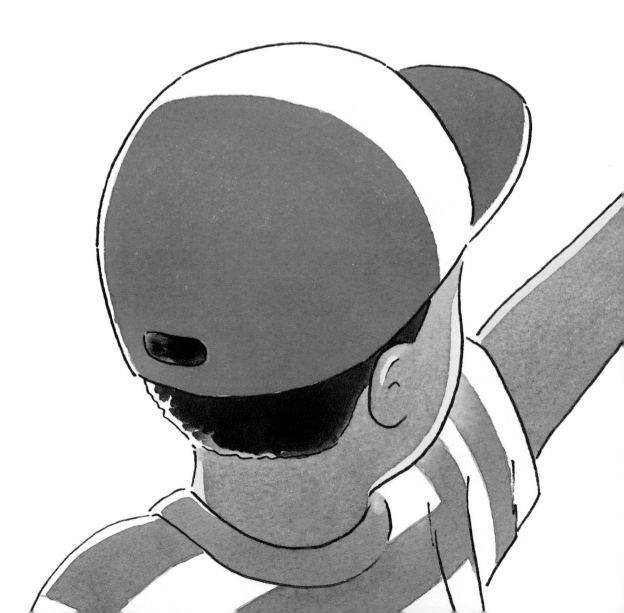

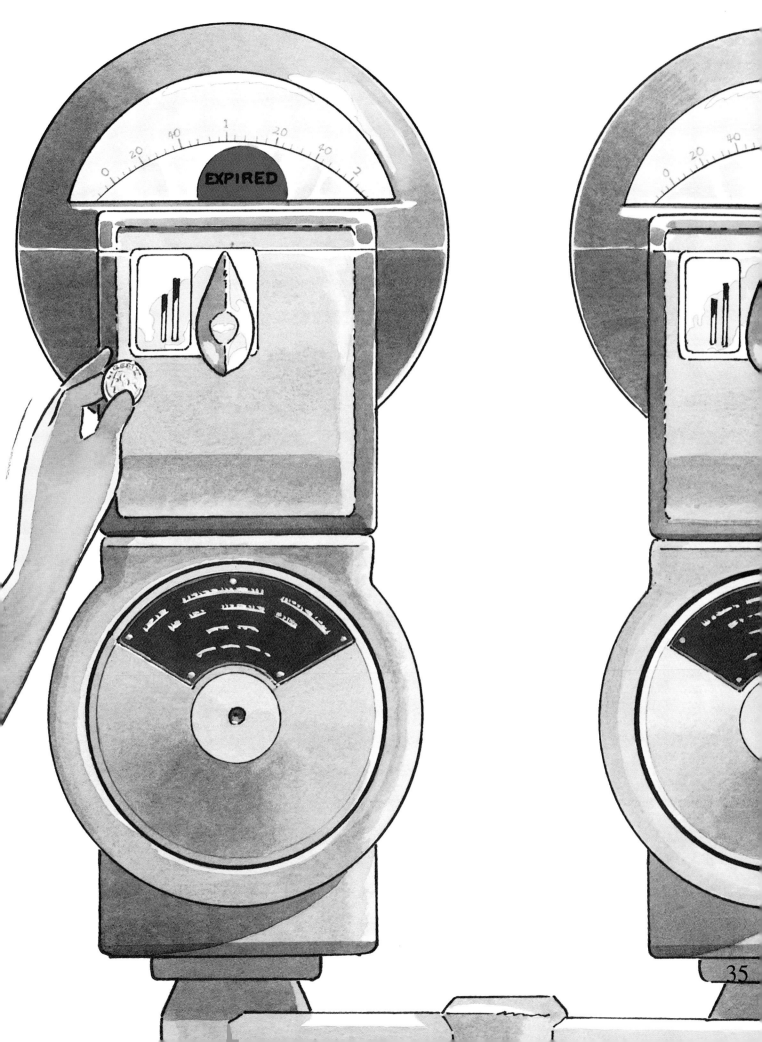

Why are there so many stores?

Because people in your neighborhood need so many different things. Shopping is easiest when there are lots of stores close together. In different stores you can shop for clothes, toys, books, flowers, and food. You can also get your hair cut, rent a video, or put money in a bank.

37

Why do banks have so much money?

People put money in the bank to keep it safe. They can also store valuable things like jewelry in a special locked room called a vault.

Banks give customers pieces of paper called checks. People can write checks to take money out of the bank, or to pay for things they buy at other places.

39

Where do you shop for food in the city?

A city neighborhood has lots of places to buy food. Small markets sell fresh fruits and vegetables. Other stores sell fish and meat. In a delicatessen you can buy sandwiches that are ready to eat. You may even buy a hot dog or a pretzel from an open pushcart on the street corner!

Why do bakeries smell so nice?

Because the ovens are full of delicious things to eat! A baker mixes flour, sugar, butter, and eggs to make a batter. He uses different batters to make bread, cookies, and cakes. While they are baking, the store fills with wonderful smells. When the baked goods come out of the oven, the baker brings them to the front of the bakery to sell to his lucky customers.

How is an apartment building different from a house?

An apartment building is a bit like a neighborhood. Inside are many families, each living in its own apartment. Like a house, an apartment has a kitchen, a bathroom, and other rooms for living and sleeping. People who live in an apartment have neighbors above the ceiling, below the floor, and right next door!

45

What makes a neighborhood special?

Every neighborhood is a place where people live, work, and play together. Even so, each neighborhood is a one-of-a-kind place. Your family, friends, and neighbors make it that way. Your neighborhood is where you learn things and grow every day. It is a special place that you will remember forever.

TIME-LIFE for CHILDREN®

Managing Editor: Patricia Daniels
Editorial Directors: Jean Burke Crawford, Allan Fallow,
Karin Kinney, Sara Mark
Senior Art Director: Susan K. White
Publishing Associate: Marike van der Veen
Administrative Assistant: Mary M. Saxton
Production Manager: Marlene Zack
Senior Copyeditor: Colette Stockum
Quality Assurance Manager: Miriam Newton
Library: Louise D. Forstall, Anne Heising

Special Contributor: Barbara Klein
Researcher: Fran Kalavritinos
Writer: Andrew Gutelle

Designed by: David Bennett Books

Series design: David Bennett
Book design: David Bennett
Art direction: David Bennett
Illustrated by: Peter Wingham
Additional cover illustrations by: Nick Baxter

First printing. Printed in U.S.A.
Published simultaneously in Canada.

Time Life Inc. is a wholly owned subsidiary of THE TIME INC. BOOK COMPANY.

TIME-LIFE is a trademark of Time Warner Inc. U.S.A.
For subscription information, call 1-800-621-7026.

School and library distribution by Time-Life Education,
P.O. Box 85026, Richmond, VA 23285-5026

Library of Congress Cataloging-in-Publication Data

Who named my street Magnolia? : first questions and answers about neighborhoods.
p. cm.—(Library of first questions and answers)
ISBN 0-7835-0898-0 (hardcover)
1. Neighborhood—Juvenile literature. 2. Community—Juvenile literature. [1. Neighborhood—Miscellanea.
2. Community Life—Miscellanea. 3. Questions and answers.] I. Time-Life for Children (Firm) II. Series.
HM131. W455 1995
94-22371
307.3'362—dc20
CIP
AC

Consultants

Dr. Lewis P. Lipsitt, an internationally recognized specialist on childhood development, was the 1990 recipient of the Nicholas Hobbs Award for science in the service of children. He has served as the science director for the American Psychological Association and is a professor of psychology and medical science at Brown University.

Dr. Judith A. Schickedanz, an authority on the education of preschool children, is an associate professor of early childhood education at the Boston University School of Education, where she also directs the Early Childhood Learning Laboratory. Her published work includes *More Than the ABCs: Early Stages of Reading and Writing Development* as well as several textbooks and many scholarly papers.